Writer's Choice
Grammar and Composition

Grammar Practice
Workbook

Grade 6

Glencoe
McGraw-Hill

New York, New York   Columbus, Ohio   Woodland Hills, California   Peoria, Illinois

Glencoe/McGraw-Hill

A Division of The **McGraw·Hill** Companies

Send all inquiries to:
Glencoe/McGraw-Hill
8787 Orion Place
Columbus, Ohio 43240

ISBN 0-07-823352-6

5 6 7 8 9   024   09 08 07 06 05

Contents

Contents

Name .... Class .... Date ....

8.1–2   Sentences and Sentence Fragments

Key Information

A **sentence** expresses a complete thought. All sentences begin with a capital letter and end with a punctuation mark. A **declarative sentence** tells or states something. It ends with a period. An **interrogative sentence** asks a question. It ends with a question mark. An **exclamatory sentence** expresses a strong feeling. It ends with an exclamation point. An **imperative sentence** commands someone to do something. It ends with a period.

A sentence must have both a **subject** and a **predicate** in order to express a complete thought. The subject names *whom* or *what* the sentence is about. The predicate tells what the subject *does* or what it is *like*.

   Dr. Seuss (subject) wrote children's books. (predicate)

A group of words that lacks either a subject, a predicate, or both is called a **sentence fragment.** Avoid sentence fragments when you write.

■ A. Punctuating Sentences Correctly

Rewrite each sentence, adding capital letters and end punctuation where needed. Then indicate whether the sentence is *declarative, interrogative, exclamatory,* or *imperative.*

1. do you know how to blow bubbles _____

_____

2. tell me about your biggest bubble _____

_____

3. my cousin once blew a bubble as big as a cabbage_____

_____

4. what a great bubble that was _____

_____

■ B. Forming Complete Sentences

Correct these sentence fragments by adding words to make complete sentences. Remember to start each sentence with a capital letter and end it with the proper punctuation.

1. two small dogs _____

2. gave me a present_____

3. she always_____

4. I sometimes _____

Name .... Class .... Date ....

| **8.3** | **Subjects and Predicates** |

Key Information

The **complete subject** of a sentence includes all the words in the subject.

   The whole class visited the museum.

The **complete predicate** of a sentence includes all the words in the predicate.

   The whole class **visited the museum.**

The **simple subject** is the main word or group of words in the complete subject.

   The whole **class** visited the museum.

The **simple predicate** is the main word or group of words in the complete predicate.

   The whole class **visited** the museum.

■ **A. Identifying Complete Subjects and Complete Predicates**

Underline each complete subject once, and underline each complete predicate twice.

1. My cousin visited South America last year.

2. She took a boat ride up the Amazon River.

3. The Amazon is the largest river in the world.

4. The river flows just south of the Equator.

5. The weather was hot and humid.

6. It rained almost every day.

7. Over fifteen hundred species of fish live in the Amazon.

8. The jungle grows right up to the water's edge.

9. She saw many exotic birds.

10. Her favorite was the toucan.

■ **B. Identifying Simple Subjects and Simple Predicates**

Underline each simple subject once and each simple predicate twice.

1. Her younger brother took lots of photos.

2. His favorite photograph shows a giant butterfly.

3. He always kept his camera with him.

4. Several people asked him about his camera.

5. Once, the boat stopped at a small fishing village.

6. He got some good pictures of people at work.

Name .... Class .... Date ....

8.4 Finding Subjects

> **Key Information**
>
> Understanding word order can help you identify the parts of a sentence. Most statements begin with the subject.
>
> **Jim Henson** created the Muppet puppets.
>
> Questions can begin with part or all of the predicate, followed by the subject and the rest of the predicate.
>
> **Did** Jim Henson **create the Muppet puppets?**
>
> You can find the subject of a question by rearranging the sentence into a statement.
>
> **Jim Henson** did create the Muppet puppets.
>
> Statements sometimes present the predicate before the subject.
>
> **Out of nowhere came** the answer.
>
> Imperative sentences (requests or commands) usually have an unstated subject. The word *you* is understood to be the subject.

■ A. Rewriting Questions as Statements

Rewrite each question as a statement. Underline each simple subject.

1. Did Robin Hood really take from the rich and give to the poor? _____

_____

2. Was Sherwood Forest a safe place to hide?_____

_____

3. Were the soldiers able to capture him?_____

_____

4. Did Robin escape? _____

_____

■ B. Finding Subjects

Underline each subject. Write *(You)* before the sentence with an understood subject.

_____ **1.** Tell me another story.

_____ **2.** On the log stood Little John.

_____ **3.** Both men fell into the river.

_____ **4.** Out of the forest galloped the sheriff.

_____ **5.** Was Robin Hood a good leader?

8.5 Compound Subjects and Compound Predicates

Key Information

A compound subject has two or more subjects that have the same predicate. The subjects are joined by the words *and* or *or.*

> **Julia** *and* **Ramon** worked in the bakery.

A compound predicate has two or more verbs with the same subject. The verbs are joined by the words *and, or,* or *but.*

> Juan **worked** in the store *and* **delivered** newspapers.

Some sentences have both a compound subject and a compound predicate.

> **Julia** *and* **Ramon worked** in the bakery *but* **found** time for piano lessons.

■ A. Identifying Compound Subjects and Compound Predicates

Underline the subjects and predicates within each compound subject and compound predicate. Some sentences contain both a compound subject and a compound predicate.

1. Robin Hood and Little John ran from the soldiers.

2. Robin started a fire and told this story.

3. Robin, John, and Friar Tuck became the best of friends.

4. The sheriff called him an outlaw and ordered his arrest.

5. In the end, King Richard pardoned Robin, gave him back his land, and made him a knight.

6. Robin Hood and Little John robbed from the rich and gave to the poor.

7. Were the prince and the sheriff greedy?

8. Sherwood Forest gave them shelter and provided food.

■ B. Using Compound Subjects and Compound Predicates

Imagine that you and your friends were part of Robin's Merry Men. Write five sentences about the things you would do on a typical day. Use a compound subject, a compound predicate, or both in each of your sentences.

_____

_____

_____

_____

_____

Name .... **Class** .... **Date** ....

| 8.6 | **Simple, Compound, and Complex Sentences** |

Key Information

A **compound sentence** contains two or more simple sentences. Each simple sentence in a compound sentence is called a **main clause.** A clause contains a subject and a predicate.

> **Karen hurried,** but **Emil walked slowly.** (two main clauses joined by a conjunction)

A **complex sentence** has one main clause and one or more **subordinate clauses**—clauses that cannot stand alone.

> Karen hurried **because she was late.** (main clause and subordinate clause introduced by subordinating conjunction *because.*)

A **run-on sentence** is two or more sentences incorrectly written as one. To correct a run-on, write it as two sentences, or join the clauses with a comma and a conjunction.

■ A. Identifying Simple, Compound, and Complex Sentences

Write whether each sentence is *simple, compound,* or *complex.*

1. George and James stayed at a ranch last summer. _____

2. George liked getting up early, but James slept late. _____

3. George had finished his chores before he ate breakfast. _____

4. They slept in the bunkhouse, which was near the kitchen. _____

5. James rode horses after breakfast; George helped the rancher. _____

6. George brushed the horses each morning and night. _____

■ B. Correcting Run-on Sentences

Correct the following run-on sentences.

1. Maria looked around Laurie ran. _____

_____

2. The school closed for the summer we were happy. _____

_____

3. The bus turned left the car went straight. _____

_____

4. The movie ended we went home. _____

_____

Name .... Class .... Date ....

| **9.1** | **Common and Proper Nouns** |

Key Information

A noun names a person, place, thing, or idea.

Persons	**Places**	**Things**	**Ideas**
artist	desert	fire	loyalty
singer	country	leaf	happiness

A **common noun** is a general name for *any* person, place, thing, or idea.

A **proper noun** names a *particular* person, place, thing, or idea. Proper nouns can consist of more than one word. You should capitalize the first word and all other important words in a proper noun.

Common Nouns	**Proper Nouns**
poet	William Blake
country	Thailand
play	*Romeo and Juliet*

■ A. Identifying Nouns

Underline each noun in the sentences that follow. There are one or more nouns in each sentence.

1. Amanda and her cousin collect stamps.

2. Her cousin has stamps from almost every country in the world.

3. Amanda has an entire book filled with stamps from America.

4. Pen pals send her stamps from their countries.

5. Her favorite stamp is from Zimbabwe.

■ B. Identifying Common and Proper Nouns

Write whether each of the following words is a common or proper noun. Correct the capitalization if necessary.

1. zoo _____

2. moscow _____

3. river _____

4. julio _____

5. lake michigan _____

6. spaniel _____

Name .... **Class** .... **Date** ....

9.2   Singular and Plural Nouns

Key Information

A **singular noun** names *one* person, place, thing, or idea. A **plural noun** names *more than one* person, place, thing, or idea.

A **collective noun** names a *group* of people or things. A collective noun is singular when the group acts as a unit. It is plural when each member of the group acts separately.

> The class goes to the museum. [singular]
> The class exchange presents with one another. [plural]

■ A. Forming Plural Nouns

Change each noun in italics to its plural form.

1. I wrapped the *glass* before I opened the *box.* _____

2. The *elf* ran after the *wolf.* _____

3. The *chief* wanted the *knife.* _____

4. The *army* fought over who would get the *turkey.* _____

5. For some strange reason, he put the *tomato* next to the *vase* on top of the *radio.*

_____

6. I keep the rabbit *hutch* behind the *shed.* _____

7. Jerry used his *camera* to take the *photo* of the *church.* _____

8. The *dancer* dropped the *mask* whenever the band played the *waltz.* _____

■ B. Using Collective Nouns

Underline each collective noun, and write whether it is singular or plural.

1. That class share their essays with one another. _____

2. Our debate team wins top honors every year. _____

3. The new band play one another's instruments. _____

4. Our family eats dinner at six. _____

5. Joanie's group outshines the rest. _____

6. Your club has too many members. _____

Name .... Class .... Date ....

| 9.3 | Possessive Nouns |

Key Information

A **possessive noun** names who or what has something.

   This is **grandfather's** watch.
   I liked the **actors'** performances.
   The **children's** room in the library is my favorite.

Remember that possessive nouns always contain apostrophes. Plural nouns that are not possessive do not.

   Have you seen the *pirate's* map? (singular possessive noun)
   I went aboard the *pirates'* ship. (plural possessive noun)
   I read about the *pirates* in school. (plural noun)

■ A. Identifying Possessive Nouns

Underline the possessive noun in each sentence, and write whether it is singular or plural.

1. I looked in the cupboard for the cat's food. _____

2. What is your brothers' favorite movie? _____

3. Did you find the boys' hiding place? _____

4. Today is Ms. Mills's birthday. _____

5. Are you the group's new president? _____

■ B. Using Singular and Plural Possessives

Write the possessive form for each word in italics.

1. I visited my *mother* workplace._____

2. Did you buy the *dog* food? _____

3. The *team* new uniforms were blue. _____

4. The *surfers* boards are on the beach. _____

5. I combed *Bess* hair carefully. _____

6. *José* new bike is a ten-speed._____

7. We watched the *soldiers* trucks leave. _____

8. Do you still have your *cousin* phone number? _____

Name .... Class .... Date ....

10.1　Action Verbs and Direct Objects

Key Information

An **action verb** names an action in one or more words.

> looks　　reaches　　will remember　　speak　　suggest

A **direct object** is a noun that receives the action of a verb. It answers the question *whom* or *what* after an action verb.

> We should tip the **waiter.** [The direct object, *waiter,* tells us whom we should tip.]

Transitive verbs have direct objects. **Intransitive** verbs do not have direct objects.

> Maria **drives** a green sports car. [transitive]
> Maria **drives** carefully. [intransitive]

■ A. Identifying Action Verbs and Direct Objects

Underline the action verbs once and underline the direct objects twice. Some verbs may not have a direct object.

1. Ginny plays piano in a band.

2. Hamsters sleep during the day.

3. My parents both work for the same company.

4. Jordan explored the reefs for coral.

5. I finished dinner before my brother.

6. Joanie found a dollar.

7. The cat caught the mouse.

8. Delores chased the train.

9. My parents wrote a note.

10. Karen put the book back.

■ B. Writing Sentences with Action Verbs and Direct Objects

Write four sentences about things you and your friends often do. Use an action verb and a direct object in each sentence.

1. _____

2. _____

3. _____

4. _____

Name .... Class .... Date ....

10.2   Indirect Objects

> **Key Information**
>
> In a sentence with an action verb, an **indirect object** tells us *to whom* or *for whom* an action was done.
>
>   The children sang their **parents** a new song.
>
> In this sentence, the indirect object *parents* tells *to whom* the children sang.
>
> An indirect object appears only in sentences that contain a direct object, and the indirect object always comes before the direct object. You can add the word *to* or *for* before the indirect object and change its position in the sentence without changing the meaning of the sentence.

■ A. Distinguishing Between Direct and Indirect Objects

Write whether the words in italics are direct objects or indirect objects.

1. I gave Maria a new *pen*. _____

2. Did you write your *cousins* a letter? _____

3. Dave brought *Henrietta* some flowers. _____

4. The band wrote three new *songs*. _____

5. Give *José* my share. _____

■ B. Identifying Direct and Indirect Objects

Underline the direct object once and underline the indirect object twice in each of these sentences.

1. Banks lend people money for buying new homes.

2. The class gave the teacher a present.

3. The company offered the workers new jobs.

4. Doctor Gonzalez handed Miguel and Dolores their newborn daughter.

5. Every year the mayor in the village grants the people one request.

6. The store offered the shoppers lower prices.

7. The contractors built my family a new kitchen.

8. Public television offers viewers many programs.

9. The librarian read the children three stories.

10. We gave our parents gifts for their anniversary.

Name .... Class .... Date ....

| **10.4** | **Present, Past, and Future Tenses** |

Key Information

Verb **tenses** reveal *when* something happens. The **present tense** of a verb names an action that happens regularly. It can also express a general truth.

> I **talk** to her every day.

The **past tense** of a verb names an action that has already happened.

> I **talked to** her yesterday.

The **future tense** names an action that will take place in the future. The future tense is formed by adding the helping verb *will* or *shall* to the base form of the verb.

> I **shall talk** to her later.
> The Browns **will visit** Washington, D.C., in the spring.

■ A. Identifying Present, Past, and Future Tenses

Underline each verb, and write whether it is in the *present, past,* or *future* tense.

1. We watched the parade on New Year's Day. _____

2. Tomorrow I shall finish this puzzle. _____

3. Jorge fishes with his uncle. _____

4. I first met Cheryl at the library. _____

5. They will pass this way. _____

6. The otter washed its food carefully. _____

7. Robert Cray plays guitar. _____

8. Kevin will catch the ball. _____

■ B. Using Present, Past, and Future Tenses

Write the form of the verb asked for in parentheses.

1. I (past of *visit*) my grandparents. _____

2. Julio (future of *act*) in the play. _____

3. Whales (present of *live*) in the ocean. _____

4. Maria (past of *return*) my tapes. _____

5. The box (present of *contain*) three surprises. _____

6. My parents (future of *bring*) the dessert. _____

7. Teresa and her sister (past of *discuss*) their choices. _____

8. The porpoise (present of *jump)* through the hoop. _____

Name .... Class .... Date ....

10.5 Main Verbs and Helping Verbs

Key Information

Verbs have four principal parts.

Base Form	Present Participle	Past Form	Past Participle
talk	talking	talked	talked
play	playing	played	played

These principal parts are often used with a **helping verb** to form a **verb phrase**. A **verb phrase** is one or more helping verbs followed by the main verb.

We **have been studying** for a test.

A **helping verb** is a verb that helps the main verb tell about an action or make a statement.

Forms of the verb *be* and *have* are the most commonly used helping verbs.

Forms of *be* are often used with the present participle.

I **am** talking.

Forms of *have* are often used with the past participle.

She **has** talked.

■ A. Identifying Helping Verbs and Main Verbs

Underline the verb phrase once, and underline the main verb twice.

1. I was looking in the closet.

2. Maria has missed the bus.

3. The students were talking loudly.

4. The cold weather had begun.

5. Firefighters have helped people for years.

6. I am trying my best.

7. We are relying on each other.

8. Our family was traveling during December.

■ B. Identifying Past and Present Participles

Underline the verb phrase and write whether the main verb is a present participle or a past participle.

1. The workers were improving the road. _____

2. I am working on my math. _____

3. Caroline was feeding her cat. _____

4. The mechanic had repaired the truck. _____

5. You have tried everything now. _____

Name .... **Class** .... **Date** ....

10.6   Present and Past Progressive Forms

> **Key Information**
>
> The **present progressive form** of a verb tells about an action that is continuing now. It consists of the present participle and the helping verb *am, is,* or *are.*
>
>   The students **are talking** to one another.
>
> The **past progressive form** of a verb names an action that continued for some time in the past. It consists of the present participle and the helping verb *was* or *were.*
>
>   The students **were talking** for hours.

■ A. Using the Present Progressive Form

Write the present progressive form of the verb in parentheses.

1. My basketball team (sell) candy. _____

2. We (raise) money for new uniforms. _____

3. My father (help) us by providing transportation. _____

4. He (drive) us around town. _____

5. We (hope) to raise enough for new shoes. _____

6. Other teams (try) to help. _____

7. The football team (play) an exhibition game. _____

8. You (carry) a heavy load. _____

■ B. Using the Past Progressive Form

Write the past progressive form of the verb in parentheses.

1. I (sing) in the choir. _____

2. Jimmy (play) in my band. _____

3. After the concert, the crowd (call) for more. _____

4. Saturday, I (look) for a new guitar. _____

5. Because of the holiday, the stores (close) early. _____

6. You (walk) with me. _____

7. We (talk) about our favorite songs. _____

8. I (think) about buying a Gibson. _____

Name .... Class .... Date ....

10.7　Perfect Tenses

> **Key Information**
>
> The **present perfect tense** of a verb tells about something that happened at an indefinite time in the past. It also tells about an action that happened in the past and is still happening now. This tense consists of the helping verb *have* or *has* followed by the past participle of the main verb.
>
> My father **has driven** station wagons for many years.
>
> The **past perfect tense** names an action that took place before another action or event in the past. This tense consists of the helping verb *had* and the past participle of the main verb.
>
> Until he traded it in, my father **had driven** that station wagon for ten years.

■ A. Distinguishing Tenses

Underline the verb or verb phrase. Write whether it is in the *present, past, present perfect,* or *past perfect* tense.

1. Eagles live in these mountains. _____

2. They have lived here for centuries. _____

3. For years I had looked for one. _____

4. I never saw an eagle. _____

5. My parents had helped me. _____

6. I have watched every day for weeks. _____

■ B. Using the Perfect Tenses

Underline the verbs in these sentences. Change the present tense verbs to the present perfect tense; change the past tense verbs to the past perfect tense.

1. Maria read about holiday traditions. _____

2. Yogi lives in Jellystone Park. _____

3. My parents volunteer at my school. _____

4. The police officer directed traffic. _____

5. The plane flight ended early. _____

6. Maggie and George jump on the trampoline. _____

Name .... Class .... Date ....

10.8–9 Irregular Verbs

Key Information

The **past** and **past participle** forms of **irregular verbs** are not formed by adding *-ed*.

For some irregular verbs one vowel changes to form the **past** and **past participle.**
 Base: begin **Past:** began **Past Participle:** begun

For some irregular verbs the **past** and **past participle** are the same.
 Base: sit **Past:** sat **Past Participle:** sat

For a few verbs the **base** form and the **past participle** are the same.
 Base: run **Past:** ran **Past Participle:** run

For some verbs the **past** form ends in *-ew* and the **past participle** in *-wn.*
 Base: know **Past:** knew **Past Participle:** known

Some **past participles** end in *-en.*
 Base: write **Past:** wrote **Past Participle:** written

For some verbs the **past** and the **past participle** do not follow a pattern.
 Base: go **Past:** went **Past Participle:** gone

For a few verbs the **base** form, the **past** form, and the **past participle** are the same.
 Base: put **Past:** put **Past Participle:** put

■ A. Using the Past Tense of Irregular Verbs

Write the past tense form of the verb in parentheses.

1. My brother (drink) three glasses of milk today._____

2. I (swim) twelve laps this morning._____

3. Consuela (know) everyone in town. _____

4. I (teach) guitar to young children. _____

5. I (tear) my sleeve on that nail. _____

6. My dad (drive) by the park. _____

■ B. Using the Past Participle of Irregular Verbs

Write the past participle of the verb in parentheses.

1. I have (feel) a little ill lately. _____

2. She has (do) all her chores. _____

3. Have you (write) your essay yet? _____

4. Jeremy has (fell) again._____

5. Julia has (grew) tomatoes for years. _____

6. I have (run) three races today. _____

Name .... Class .... Date ....

| 11.1–2 | **Using Pronouns Correctly** |

Key Information

A **pronoun** is a word that takes the place of one or more nouns and the words that describe those nouns. Pronouns that are used to refer to people or things are called **personal pronouns.**

Roland has a favorite song. **He** sings **it** often.

Remember to use a **subject pronoun** in place of the subject of a sentence and an **object pronoun** in place of the direct or indirect object of a verb.

They grow many kinds of vegetables. (subject)
We gave **them** some new seeds. (indirect object)
The gift surprised **them.** (direct object)

Compound subjects and **compound objects** follow the same rules.

The band and I rode on the bus. (subject—not *The band and me*)
The audience liked **the band and me.** (object—not *the band and I*)

■ A. Using Subject and Object Pronouns Correctly

Circle the correct pronoun in each sentence.

1. (Her, She) likes to ride the train.

2. Dad helped (us, we) with our chores.

3. My uncles wanted to help, but (they, them) were too tired.

4. The coach told (they, them) to try harder.

■ B. Using Subject and Object Pronouns

In the space provided, write the pronoun that correctly replaces the underlined words.

1. Ms. Chou is a librarian in my town. <u>Ms. Chou</u> reads stories every Saturday. _____

2. All the kids from our neighborhood admire <u>Ms. Chou</u>. _____

3. <u>All the kids</u> like the stories Ms. Chou reads. _____

4. Jimmy is always there. <u>Jimmy</u> helps <u>Ms. Chou</u> after the reading session. _____

■ C. Using Compound Subject and Compound Object Pronouns

Write the correct pronoun for each of the underlined words.

1. Jessica and <u>Jason</u> liked to play volleyball. _____

2. I sent <u>Margaret</u> and <u>her friends</u> my new address. _____

3. Julio and <u>Catherine</u> thought football was dangerous. _____

4. <u>The younger kids</u> and I went outside. _____

Name .... Class .... Date ....

11.3   Pronouns and Antecedents

Key Information

A pronoun always refers to a noun. That noun is the pronoun's **antecedent.**

    Jeremy found a stray cat. **He** took **it** home.

(*Jeremy* is the antecedent of *He. Cat* is the antecedent of *it.*)

Pronouns must agree with their antecedents in number and gender. The gender of a noun may be feminine, masculine, or neuter.

    Harry liked **math and science. He** always did well in **them.**
    (*He* agrees with *Harry* in number—singular—and gender—masculine. *Them* agrees with *math and science*—plural and neuter.)

A pronoun must clearly refer to its antecedent.

    My rabbits share a cage with several hamsters. **They** are always hungry.

(Does *they* refer to *rabbits* or to *hamsters?* The pronoun reference is unclear.)

If the pronoun can refer to more than one noun, avoid using a pronoun at all.

■ A. Identifying Antecedents

Underline once the personal pronoun in the second sentence that refers to a noun in the first. Underline twice the antecedent in the first sentence.

1. My father and I went camping in the desert. We took a walk the first night out.

2. The stars seemed brighter than back home. They seemed so bright because we were in the desert, far away from city lights.

3. Jack went back and got out the telescope. It was brand new.

4. My father told me to look toward the east. He pointed at a light streaking across the sky.

■ B. Using Pronouns with Their Antecedents

Write the correct pronoun for the underlined antecedent.

    Example: <u>Jeremy</u> read <u>his report</u> to the class.
    He read it to the class.

1. <u>People</u> were decorating the town for the parade. _____

2. Cathy gave <u>Dorothy</u> a drum set. _____

3. My brother watches <u>the same television shows</u> every day. _____

4. Gayatri brought <u>her puppet</u> to the story hour for children. _____

5. <u>Gabriela and her sister</u> wore matching skirts. _____

Name .... Class .... Date ....

11.4 Possessive Pronouns

Key Information

A **possessive pronoun** names a person or thing that has something. A possessive pronoun does not contain an apostrophe. Some possessive pronouns appear before a noun and replace the name of the person or thing that has something.

Julian's group is finished. **His** group is finished.

Other possessive pronouns stand alone in a sentence.

Mine is the red one. The one on the table is **yours.**

Don't confuse the possessive pronoun *its* with the contraction *it's* (it is).

Its colors had faded. (possessive pronoun)
It's beginning to fade. (contraction)

■ A. Identifying Possessive Pronouns

Underline the possessive pronouns in the sentences below, and write them in the space provided.

1. Michael dropped his ice cream on the ground. _____
2. Several people claimed the prize was theirs. _____
3. Susan and Hussain closed their eyes when Kelly brought out the cake. _____
4. We couldn't decide which of the cars was ours. _____
5. Our track team took first place. _____
6. Do you have my tapes? _____
7. She was looking for her books. _____
8. Does Kelly's watch show the same time as yours? _____
9. I got mine before you did. _____
10. The dog lost its collar. _____

■ B. Using Possessive Pronouns Correctly

Write the correct word from the parentheses in each sentence.

1. Please see if (you're, your) painting is dry. _____
2. (It's, Its) too early to go to the show. _____
3. (They're, Their) latest record is selling well. _____
4. I wonder if (you're, your) brother will go with me. _____
5. Did the dog lose (it's, its) collar? _____

Name .... **Class** .... **Date** ....

11.5   Indefinite Pronouns

Key Information

An **indefinite pronoun** does not refer to a particular person, place, or thing.

> **Anything** is possible.

Some indefinite pronouns are always singular. Some indefinite pronouns are always plural. Other indefinite pronouns can be singular or plural, depending on the phrase that follows.

If you use an indefinite pronoun as the subject of a sentence, the verb must agree with it in number.

> **Both are** available. (plural)
> **Neither is** available. (singular)
> **Some** of the movie **is** boring. (singular)
> **Some** of the movies **are** boring. (plural)

■ A. Identifying Indefinite Pronouns

Write the indefinite pronoun in parentheses that correctly completes the sentence.

1. (Everybody, Few) knows how to dance. _____

2. Every evening (nobody, both) go home. _____

3. (Many, Everyone) remember their lessons. _____

4. (Each, Both) of the children puts on mittens. _____

■ B. Using Indefinite Pronouns Correctly

Write the word in parentheses that correctly completes the sentence.

1. Each of the chairs in this room (are, is) made of wood. _____

2. Most of the children (leave, leaves) books on the table._____

3. Some of the animals wash (their, its) food before eating. _____

4. Each has (their, its) own special place to sleep. _____

■ C. Writing with Indefinite Pronouns

Write four sentences of your own that use indefinite pronouns as subjects. The verbs you use must agree in number with the subjects.

1. _____

2. _____

3. _____

4. _____

Name .... Class .... Date ....

12.1 Adjectives and Proper Adjectives

Key Information

An **adjective** is a word that describes a noun or a pronoun.

> Harry listens to **classical** music. **[What kind?]**
> I bought **three** apples. **[How many?)**
> Ira sent me **that** picture. **[Which one?]**

Predicate adjectives follow linking verbs and modify the subject of a sentence.

> Moira's house is **beautiful.**

Proper adjectives are formed from proper nouns and start with a capital letter. Some proper adjectives are formed by adding an ending to the noun form.

> **Navajo** blanket [simple noun form]   **African art** [ending added]

■ A. Identifying Adjectives

Underline each adjective once and the noun it modifies twice.

1. Emily avoided the large dog.

2. Its bark sounded ferocious.

3. Later, Emily met the young owner of the dog.

4. The dog was harmless.

5. Emily and the dog became good friends.

6. Sometimes, dogs are nervous, and they bark.

■ B. Identifying Proper Adjectives

Write each proper adjective, using correct capitalization. Then write any other adjective in the sentence.

1. The vacations were at different american campgrounds. _____

2. Henrietta stayed on a navajo reservation with close friends. _____

3. Marcus spent two months on the virginia coast. _____

4. Good friends visited the peruvian mountains. _____

5. They brought back several pieces of incan art. _____

6. We studied african wildlife in a science class. _____

Name .... Class .... Date ....

12.2 Articles and Demonstratives

Key Information

The words *a, an,* and *the* are special kinds of adjectives called **articles.** Use *the* to point out a particular item or items.

> Marmosets are **the** smallest monkey.

Use *a* or *an* to point out one item in a group. *A* appears before words that begin with a consonant sound. *An* appears before words that begin with a vowel sound.

> **A** marmoset can fit in **an** adult's hand.

This, that, these, and *those* are **demonstrative adjectives.** They point out specific things.

> **This** book is well written.

This, that, these, and *those* can also stand alone in a sentence as **demonstrative pronouns** (subjects or objects).

> **This** is my bag of marbles.
> Bring **those** along.

■ A. Using Articles

For each sentence, underline the correct article in parentheses.

  1. Ms. Rodriguez is (a, an) science teacher.

  2. Have you had her for (a, the) teacher?

  3. Some kids say she is the hardest teacher in (a, the) school.

  4. She gives (a, an) exam every week.

  5. I think she is (a, an) good teacher.

  6. Her class is hard, but she makes science (a, the) fun subject.

■ B. Using Demonstratives

For each sentence, underline the correct demonstrative word in parentheses.

  1. I recently saw (that, those) movie.

  2. It was showing at (that, those) new theater.

  3. I went with (that, those) kids from school.

  4. (This, These) actors play their parts well.

  5. (This, These) was the third film I've seen starring Mel Gibson.

  6. He had the best role in (this, these) film.

Name .... Class .... Date ....

| 12.3 | **Adjectives That Compare** |

Key Information

Use the **comparative** form of an adjective to compare two things. You usually form the comparative for short adjectives by adding -*er* to the adjective.

Whales are **bigger** than elephants.

You usually add *more* before the adjective to form the comparative form of adjectives with two or more syllables.

Are whales **more intelligent** than elephants?

Use the **superlative** form of an adjective to compare more than two things.

Add -*est* to short adjectives to form the superlative.

Whales are the **biggest** animals on Earth.

Add the word **most** before longer adjectives.

Are whales the **most intelligent** animals?

■ A. Choosing the Comparative or Superlative Form

Underline the correct form of the adjective in the parentheses.

1. Amanda is the (faster, fastest) runner I know.

2. Ronald used to be (faster, fastest) than Amanda.

3. Now Ronald tries (harder, hardest) than before.

4. Good sportsmanship is (most important, more important) than winning.

5. I like to run when it is (colder, coldest) than today.

6. Amanda wants to be (most famous, more famous) than any other runner.

■ B. Using the Comparative and Superlative Forms

Write the correct comparative or superlative form of the adjective in parentheses.

1. That play was (difficult) to understand than the others. _____

2. August is the (warm) month of the year. _____

3. Karen's gift was the (thoughtful) of all. _____

4. This river is (muddy) than the Mississippi. _____

5. My brother's hair is (curly) than mine. _____

6. That test was the (difficult) of all. _____

7. Yesterday's game was (exciting) than last week's. _____

8. This book is (easy) to read than that one. _____

Name .... Class .... Date ....

13.1   Adverbs Modifying Verbs

Key Information

Adverbs are words that describe or modify verbs. Adverbs answer the questions *how, when,* or *where.*

> Jaime plays **skillfully.** [how]   Jaime plays **outside.** [where]
> Jaime plays **often.** [when]

When used to modify a verb, an adverb may appear *before the verb, after the verb, at the beginning of the sentence,* or *at the end of the sentence.*

> Jaime **later** played with the band. [before the verb]
> Jaime played **later** with the band. [after the verb]
> **Later** Jaime played with the band. [beginning of sentence]
> Jaime played with the band **later.** [end of sentence]

Most adverbs are formed by adding *-ly* to adjectives: **carefully, usually, nearly.**

■ A. Identifying Adverbs

In the space provided, write the adverb in each sentence. Then underline the word or words the adverb modifies.

1. Our teacher always wins. _____

2. The class debated loudly. _____

3. My parents built a playroom downstairs. _____

4. Outside I could hear their laughter. _____

5. I almost missed the train. _____

■ B. Using Adverbs

Rewrite each sentence, adding an adverb that modifies the verb in the sentence.

1. We arrived at the theater. _____

2. Jeffrey asked me. _____

3. You and I moved. _____

4. My two friends go there. _____

5. The Joyces accepted our invitation. _____

6. She gave me permission. _____

7. She gave me the gifts. _____

8. They volunteered. _____

Name .... **Class** .... **Date** ....

| **13.2** | **Adverbs Modifying Adjectives and Adverbs** |

Key Information

Adverbs can be used to modify adjectives and adverbs. Notice how the adverb modifies the adjective in the sentence below.

> Jim Henson created a group of **very** unusual puppets.

The adverb *very* tells us how unusual the puppets were. Adverbs can also be used to modify other adverbs.

> His puppet creations have worked **very** successfully.
> Their appearance on *Sesame Street* increased their popularity **quite** rapidly.

Adverbs that modify adjectives and other adverbs almost always appear directly before the word they modify.

■ A. Identifying Adverbs

Underline the word that the adverb in italics modifies. Tell whether the modified word is a *verb, adjective,* or *adverb.*

1. I have a *very* remarkable family. _____

2. My uncle is an *extremely* tall man. _____

3. Trisha, my sister, learns new subjects *quite* easily. _____

4. My brother Kevin has been our starting pitcher for *nearly* three years._____

5. My father *always* wins town elections. _____

6. Mom got her job *almost* immediately following college. _____

7. My kid brother runs *very* quickly. _____

8. I *often* write stories. _____

■ B. Using Adverbs

Rewrite each sentence, adding an adverb to modify the word in italics. Try to use a different adverb each time.

1. Jorge *looked* behind the door._____

2. The large orange cat *slept* on the couch. _____

3. The river rose *quickly.*_____

4. Back on the ranch, Jimmy rode the *wild* horse. _____

5. I got up *late* this morning. _____

Name .... Class .... Date ....

13.3   Adverbs That Compare

Key Information

Use the **comparative** form of an adverb to compare two actions. For adverbs of only one syllable, add -er to form the comparative.

    Donna runs **faster** than Ricky.

Use the **superlative** form of an adverb to compare more than two actions. For adverbs of only one syllable, add -est to form the superlative.

    Donna runs the **fastest** of all.

For adverbs that end in -ly or have more than one syllable, use more to form the comparative and most to form the superlative.

    My sandals fit **more comfortably** than my loafers.
    That is the **most brightly** colored butterfly.

Some adverbs change completely to form the comparative and superlative.

■ A. Identifying Comparative and Superlative Forms

Underline the correct form of the adverb in parentheses.

1. I arrived at the game (later, latest) than you.

2. The game promised to be the (better, best) of the year.

3. We had (less, least) to lose than the other team.

4. We played (more intelligently, most intelligently) than the Tigers.

5. One of our players ran the (faster, fastest) of anyone this year.

■ B. Making the Comparative and Superlative Forms

Write the correct form of the adverb in parentheses.

1. I like math (well) than science. _____

2. A shark swims (fast) than a man. _____

3. Mary reads (carefully) than Joseph. _____

4. Of all my friends, I like you (well). _____

5. Steve is the (much) loyal guy I know. _____

6. My mother drives (cautiously) than my dad. _____

7. Jane ran (far) than anyone else. _____

8. Did you arrive (late) than Pete? _____

Name .... Class .... Date ....

| 13.4 | **Telling Adjectives and Adverbs Apart** |

Key Information

People sometimes confuse adjectives and adverbs. It helps to look carefully at the verb.

Marvin was **careful** around the kitchen.
Marvin moved **carefully** around the kitchen.

In the first sentence, *careful* is a predicate adjective that follows the linking verb *was*. The predicate adjective modifies the subject *Marvin*. In the second sentence, *carefully* is an adverb that modifies the action verb *moved*.

Words such as *bad, real,* and *sure* are usually used as adverbs when they end in *-ly*. They are adjectives when they do not end in *-ly*. *Bad* and *good* are both adjectives. *Well* is usually an adverb, but it can be an adjective when used after a linking verb to describe a person's health or appearance: They look **well**.

■ A. Telling Adjectives and Adverbs Apart

Underline the correct word in the parentheses. Then tell whether the word you underlined is an *adjective* or *adverb*.

1. I sang (poor, poorly) last night. _____

2. The choir sings very (good, well). _____

3. Maurice moved (slow, slowly) away. _____

4. The cloud passed (silent, silently) overhead. _____

5. The sun was (bright, brightly). _____

6. I scored (good, well) on the test. _____

■ B. Using Adjectives and Adverbs Correctly

Underline the word used incorrectly in each sentence. Then write the correct form of the word in the space provided.

1. Rap is real popular. _____

2. That was a true great speech. _____

3. Jonathan dances good. _____

4. The moon shone bright through my curtain. _____

5. She plays piano real well. _____

6. My parents most never go. _____

Name .... Class .... Date ....

| 13.5 | **Avoiding Double Negatives** |

Key Information

Negative words say "no" in a sentence. The word *not* is a negative word. *Not* often appears in its shortened form, the contraction *-n't*. Affirmative words say "yes" in a sentence. Some negative and affirmative words appear below.

Negative		**Affirmative**			
not	never	ever	always	something	any
nothing	none	one	all	some	

Two negative words used in one sentence make a **double negative.** Avoid double negatives in both your writing and speaking.

Correct a double negative by removing one of the negatives or by replacing it with an affirmative word.

> incorrect: I **don't** have **nothing** to read.

> correct: I have **nothing** to read. *or* I don't have **anything** to read.

■ A. Expressing Negative Ideas

Underline the correct word in parentheses. Remember to avoid double negatives.

1. Lawrence couldn't think of (nobody, anybody) to go with him.

2. Carrie wouldn't want (no, any) help.

3. We aren't driving (nowhere, anywhere) with you.

4. Can't they have (no, any) fun?

5. We haven't (no more, any more) toys for them.

6. Maria can't take her brother (nowhere, anywhere).

■ B. Correcting Double Negatives

Rewrite the following sentences, correcting the double negatives.

1. Wasn't there no more time to play? _____

2. Larry isn't never late for school. _____

3. She doesn't want none._____

4. I don't know nothing about that. _____

5. Julia hasn't got none. _____

6. We weren't able to do nothing about it._____

7. Don't you have nothing else to do? _____

8. I haven't got no clean clothes for tomorrow. _____

Grammar Practice

Name .... Class .... Date ....

14.1–2 Prepositions and Prepositional Phrases

Key Information

A **preposition** relates a noun or pronoun to some other word in a sentence.

> We saw them **by** the theater.

A **preposition** can be more than one word.

> I sat **across from** Tom.

The **object of the preposition** is the noun or pronoun following the preposition. A **prepositional phrase** begins with the preposition and usually ends with its object.

> Marge grows tomatoes **in her garden.**

A preposition can have a compound object.

> Marge gave tomatoes **to her grandparents and her aunt.**

A sentence can have more than one prepositional phrase. A prepositional phrase can appear anywhere in a sentence.

> Marge grows tomatoes **in her garden behind the house.**
> **In her garden behind the house,** Marge grows tomatoes.

■ A. Identifying Prepositions

Underline the prepositions in each sentence.

1. All the power failed during the storm.

2. We found some candles in the drawer.

3. My brother Jan hid beneath his bed.

4. The whole house was dark except this room.

5. Shadows fell across the wall.

6. We were safe inside the basement.

■ B. Identifying Prepositions and Their Objects

Underline each prepositional phrase once. Underline the object of the preposition twice.

1. Jan was still asleep under his blanket.

2. The sun rose over the trees.

3. We walked into our yard.

4. Underneath the porch, our dog hid quietly.

5. The river had risen over its banks.

6. Water poured down our drive.

Name .... Class .... Date ....

14.3   Pronouns After Prepositions

Key Information

Use an object pronoun when the pronoun is the object of a preposition.

    Julio threw the ball past the boys.   Julio threw the ball past **them.**

Use an object pronoun when the pronoun is part of a compound object.

    Mary hit the ball past Julio and Rose.   Mary hit the ball past Julio and **her.**

To check which type of pronoun to use, say the sentence aloud with only the pronoun as the object.

    Mary hit the ball past her. [not she]

Who and *whom* are pronouns that are often confused. *Who* is a subject pronoun. *Whom* is an object pronoun.

    Who threw the ball?   To **whom** did she throw it?

■ A. Identifying Pronouns and Prepositions

Underline the prepositional phrase in each sentence. Circle the pronoun used as the object of the preposition.

1. Jeremy threw the ball past us.

2. Yesterday I got a package from them.

3. A strange dog followed behind me.

4. The parrots were screeching at you.

5. Running away from them did no good.

6. Karen took us with her this morning.

■ B. Using the Correct Pronoun

Underline the correct pronoun in parentheses.

1. My brother always walks with Mom and (I, me).

2. The floor under Tomas and (them, they) started to collapse.

3. The librarian beckoned to Cindy and (I, me).

4. Did Jackson tell you about (they, them)?

5. Jackson told you about (who, whom)?

6. Against you and (she, her), they don't stand a chance.

7. A steady rain fell on Jesse and (I, me).

8. Thunder crashed above George and (they, them).

14.4 Prepositional Phrases as Adjectives and Adverbs

Key Information

A prepositional phrase that modifies a noun or a pronoun is an **adjective phrase.** Adjective phrases can describe *subjects, direct* and *indirect objects, predicate nouns,* or *objects in other prepositional phrases.*

Shakespeare was the author **of several major plays.** [predicate noun]
Several films **of the plays** have been quite successful. [subject]

A prepositional phrase that describes a *verb,* an *adjective,* or another *adverb* is an **adverb phrase.**

Shakespeare wrote **about life and love.** [verb]
The actor was famous **for his dramatic roles.** [adjective]

■ A. Identifying Adjective and Adverb Phrases

Underline the prepositional phrase. Write whether it is an *adjective phrase* or an *adverb phrase.*

1. There were several rumors about the new kids. _____

2. The lobsters huddled against the tank. _____

3. Jeremy looked around the table. _____

4. Computers in classrooms are useful. _____

5. I write my papers in the computer lab. _____

6. Several programs for the computer are helpful. _____

7. Joshua lives east of the high school. _____

8. You are a person of many talents. _____

■ B. Using Adjective and Adverb Phrases

Write a paragraph about your favorite place. Try to use adjective or adverb phrases in each sentence. Underline the adjective and adverb phrases you use. Use additional paper if necessary.

_____

_____

_____

_____

_____

_____

_____

Name .... Class .... Date ....

| 14.5 | **Telling Prepositions and Adverbs Apart** |

Key Information

Both **prepositions** and **adverbs** can answer the questions *where?* and *when?* Some words can be used as both prepositions and adverbs. Some of these words are listed below.

through   below   out   up   in
above   over   before   near

If a word is followed closely by a noun, the word is probably a preposition, and the noun is its object.

We slept **inside our tent.**

In this sentence, *inside our tent* answers *where?* The word *inside* begins a phrase that includes the object *tent*. *Inside* is a preposition. If the word is not followed closely by a noun, then the word is probably an adverb.

When it began to rain, we went **inside.**

Here, *inside* also answers *where?*, but it does not begin a phrase. It is an adverb.

■ A. Distinguishing Between Adverbs and Prepositions

Identify the word in italics as a *preposition* or an *adverb*.

1. I left my books *outside*._____

2. Did you look *under* the desk?_____

3. Have you been here *before*?_____

4. Joey climbed *inside* the box. _____

5. I placed the fish tank carefully *on* the table._____

6. *Under* the bridge, traffic slows to a crawl. _____

■ B. Identifying Adverbs and Prepositions

Write all the adverbs and prepositions in each sentence. Write whether each word you list is a *preposition* or an *adverb*.

1. Kevin looked through the window, and then he climbed outside. _____

2. On the roof, we heard planes fly by._____

3. I looked at the snow swirling down. _____

4. Are you staying in the yard, or are you coming inside? _____

5. No one could see out through the foggy window._____

Name .... Class .... Date ....

14.6–7 Conjunctions and Interjections

Key Information

A conjunction is a word that connects words or groups of words in a sentence. The words *and, but,* and *or* are **coordinating conjunctions.** Use *and, but,* and *or* to form compound subjects, compound predicates, and compound sentences.

> Mary **and** I are both students.
> We can study at school **or** go to the library.
> I stayed at school, **but** Mary went to the library.

Pairs of conjunctions such as *either, or; neither, nor;* and *both, and* are **correlative conjunctions.**

> **Both** Mary **and** I are students.

An **interjection** is a word or group of words that expresses strong feeling. When the interjection expresses very strong feeling, it is followed by an exclamation mark.

> **Hurry!** The train is leaving now.
> **Hey,** that's mine.

■ A. Identifying Conjunctions

Underline each conjunction. Write whether it forms a *compound subject, compound predicate,* or *compound sentence.*

1. Have you seen or read about the Grand Canyon? _____

2. José and Roberta are my best friends. _____

3. Rinji looked for the book, but he couldn't find it. _____

4. The Mississippi River and the Red Sea are huge bodies of water. _____

5. Atsuko set the table, and Suzie welcomed their guests. _____

6. Perry played baseball but felt tired afterwards. _____

■ B. Identifying Interjections

Underline each interjection in the sentences below.

1. Hey! I know that guy.

2. Well, if you say so.

3. All right! I passed my history test.

4. We won. Hooray!

5. Oh, no! I can't possibly do that.

Name .... Class .... Date ....

| **15.1** | **Making Subjects and Verbs Agree** |

Key Information

A subject and its verb must *agree in number.* A singular noun subject takes a singular verb, and a plural noun subject takes a plural verb.

    This **song sounds** silly. (singular)   These **songs sound** silly. (plural)

A subject *pronoun* and its verb must also agree. Add an *-s* ending to verbs for the present tense of *she, he,* and *it.*

    I **pretend.**   She **pretends.**

The irregular verbs *be, do,* and *have* must agree with the subject whether they are used as main verbs or as helping verbs.

    He **is** the best. (main verb)   They **are** going too fast. (helping verb)
    I **do** too much. (main verb)   She **does write** well. (helping verb)

■ Identifying Subject and Verb Agreement

Underline the correct form of the verb in parentheses.

1. Moira always (finish, finishes) her homework before dinner.

2. The town clock (strike, strikes) on the hour.

3. My baby brother (say, says) "dada" and "mama."

4. The restaurants (open, opens) early on Saturdays.

5. Anthropologists (study, studies) human beings.

6. Zimbabwe (is, are) a country in Africa.

7. Trees (cover, covers) much of this land.

8. Heavy storms (cause, causes) the roads to wash out.

9. In the morning, birds (sing, sings) outside my window.

10. Josephina (play, plays) trumpet in the school band.

11. (Are, Is) you ready, Ginny?

12. All of the rides (am, are) closed today.

13. Each of the crayons (has been, have been) sharpened.

14. (Was, Were) you frightened, Tony?

15. My brother and I (is, am, are) going to the Ice Capades.

Name .... **Class** .... **Date** ....

| 15.2 | **Problems with Locating the Subject** |

Key Information

If a prepositional phrase appears between the subject and the verb in a sentence, make sure the verb agrees with the subject of the sentence and not with the object of the preposition.

The **bird** in the branches **sings** loudly.
The **birds** on that branch **sing** loudly.

Sentences that begin with *here* or *there* can fool you. Note that *here* or *there* is never the subject of the sentence. The subject will fall after the verb.

Here at the mall is my favorite **shop.**

(*Shop* is the subject. Read it as *My favorite shop is here at the mall.*)

■ A. Choosing the Right Verb Form

Underline the correct form of the verb in parentheses.

1. Some of the students in this class (has, have) extra work to do.

2. The owls in the forest (hunt, hunts) by night.

3. Three workers on this project (work, works) harder than the rest.

4. Parts of this puzzle (has, have) been lost.

5. The road through these hills (wind, winds) treacherously.

6. A carload of kids (pass, passes) by.

■ B. Identifying Subjects and Verbs

Underline the subject in each sentence. Choose the correct form of the verb in parentheses, and write it in the space provided.

1. There (is, are) three new puppies at the pet store. _____

2. Here (is, are) your new books. _____

3. There (was, were) a quiz in math today. _____

4. There (was, were) twelve questions on the quiz. _____

5. Here (is, are) my answer to that question. _____

6. There (is, are) two correct answers to that question. _____

Name .... Class .... Date ....

15.3   Agreement with Compound Subjects

Key Information

A **compound subject** consists of two or more subjects that have the same verb. The verb must agree in number with its compound subject. If the compound subject is joined by *and* or by *both . . . and,* then the verb is plural.

> Helicopters **and** jets **fly** here.
> **Both** helicopters **and** planes **use** the airport.

If the compound subject is joined by *or, nor, either . . . or,* or *neither . . . nor,* the verb agrees in number with the subject closer to it.

> A helicopter **or a** jet **flies** fast.

(*Flies* is singular because *jet* is the closer subject, and it's singular.)

> A helicopter **or** jets **fly** fast.

(*Fly* is plural because *jets* is plural.)

> **Neither** the helicopters **nor** the jet **flies** today.

(*Flies* is singular because *jet* is singular)

■ A. Identifying Compound Subjects and Their Verbs

In the following sentences, underline the compound subject once and the verb twice.

  1. Trucks and automobiles roll through our town.

  2. Jerry and Josephina play tag football with us.

  3. Both the radio and the television were on.

  4. Either the cars or the truck uses more gas.

  5. Neither the cats nor the dog was outside last night.

  6. Either the drums or the horns are too loud.

■ B. Choosing the Correct Verb Form

Underline the correct verb form in parentheses.

  1. John and I (visit, visits) my grandmother on Sundays.

  2. Both the wind and the dog (was, were) howling.

  3. Neither the players nor their mascot (seem, seems) lively today.

  4. Mom and Dad (watch, watches) each episode of this show.

  5. Either the teacher or her students (answer, answers) each question.

  6. In the forest, birds and small mammals (share, shares) resources.

Name .... Class .... Date ....

16.1–2 Using Troublesome Words

Key Information

Some words confuse people because they are very similar to other words or because they are often misused. Here are some examples:

accept and **except**

> We **accept** (take *or* receive) everything **except** (other than) the peas.

lay and **lie**

> She told us to **lay** (put *or* place) our books there and go **lie** (recline) down.

set and **sit**

> Please **set** (place *or* put) the book on the table and **sit** (be seated) down.

to, too, and **two**

> I sent the letter **to** (direction toward) Caroline **two** (number) days ago, but I used **too** (excessively) many stamps.

■ A. Choosing the Correct Word

Underline the correct word in parentheses.

1. Omar likes every vegetable (accept, except) squash.

2. Have you finished your dinner (all ready, already)?

3. Mallory thought the soup was (all together, altogether) too hot.

4. (Besides, Beside) the roast beef, was there anything else you liked?

5. After dinner, I decided to (lay, lie) down for a while.

6. Maybe Mom can (teach, learn) me how to make an apple pie.

7. Do you think the coach will (let, leave) us go with the team?

8. Jackie's jacket was too (lose, loose) on me.

■ B. Identifying the Correct Word

If the word in italics is incorrect, write the correct word. If the word is correct, write *correct*.

1. Nancy put the cereal away *between* the soup cans, the vegetables, and the juice. _____

2. The dog buried *its* bone in the backyard. _____

3. My younger brother is taller *then* yours. _____

4. Muriel thinks *they're* team is better. _____

5. That's *to* heavy for me to carry. _____

Name .... Class .... Date ....

18.1   Capitalizing Sentences, Quotations, and Salutations

Key Information

Use a capital letter to begin a sentence or a direct quotation if the quotation is a complete sentence.

    Maria whispered, "**D**on't go in there."

If the quotation is interrupted by explanatory words, don't capitalize the first word in the second part of the quotation unless that part begins another sentence.

    "Don't," Maria whispered, "**g**o in there."

"Don't go in there," Maria whispered. "**I**t's too dangerous."

Do not use a capital letter for an indirect quotation.

    Maria whispered that **w**e shouldn't go in there.

Always capitalize the first word in the salutation and in the closing of a letter.

    Dear Mr. Monroe: **Y**ours truly,

■ A. Capitalizing Sentences and Quotations

Rewrite each sentence. Correct any errors in capitalization and quotations in the sentences. If the sentence is correct, write *correct.*

1. last night, Gerry and I talked about the school play. _____

_____

2. Gerry said that he was going to try out for the lead role. _____

_____

3. "if I can learn all the lines," He said, "Ms. Rogers will let me be Peter Pan." _____

_____

4. "I will help you learn your lines," I said, "if you'll help me with mine." _____

_____

5. he handed me a copy of the play and said, "which part do you want to try for?" _____

_____

6. "Well," I answered, "If you're going to be Peter, I guess I'll be Hook." _____

_____

■ B. Capitalizing Sentences, Quotations, and Salutations

On a separate sheet of paper, write a short, informal letter to your teacher, describing a conversation you recently had with a parent or other relative. Use quotations to tell what each of you had to say. Include a salutation and closing.

Name .... Class .... Date ....

18.2   Capitalizing Names and Titles of People

Key Information

A **proper noun** names a *particular* person, place, or thing. Always capitalize a proper noun. Capitalize the names and initials of people. Capitalize a title or its abbreviation when it comes before a person's name or is used in direct address.

   Wyoming   Jackson **T**. **B**rowne   **D**r. Ali Shek

Do not capitalize a title when it follows a person's name or stands in for the name.

   Dolores Hernandez is the captain of this ship.

Capitalize the names and abbreviations of academic degrees that follow a name and the abbreviations *Jr.* and *Sr.* Capitalize words that identify family members when the words are used as titles or as substitutes for a person's name.

   Mother and **U**ncle George were the last to arrive.

■ A. Identifying Names and Titles

Underline the correct form in parentheses.

1. My friend (Dr., dr.) Thomas likes to ride the train.

2. Do you think the (doctor, Doctor) will see us soon?

3. I saw (uncle, Uncle) David last night.

4. Maria wrote an essay on (President, president) Kennedy.

5. My father's full name is Richard Davis (sr., Sr.).

■ B. Capitalizing Names and Titles

In the following sentences, circle lowercase letters that should be capitalized. If the sentence is correct, write *correct*.

1. Kevin and uncle frank went to the movies last night. _____

2. The book was written by dr. henri l. engles jr. _____

3. My adviser, mr. juntis, is the person i most admire. _____

4. Will you be traveling with captain james t. kirk? _____

5. The phone book listed her as Janet cook, ph.d. _____

6. In the first chapter, sir galahad rescues the other knights. _____

Name .... Class .... Date ....

18.3 Capitalizing Names of Places

Key Information

The names of specific places are proper nouns and are capitalized. Capitalize the names of places, such as cities, counties, states, countries, and continents.

> **S**ri **L**anka   **A**ntarctica

Capitalize the names of bodies of water and other geographical features as well as the names of parts of a country.

> **G**reat **B**arrier **R**eef   **G**obi **D**esert   the **N**orthwest   the **G**reat **P**lains

Capitalize compass points only if they name a specific part of a country. Do not capitalize adjectives that merely show direction.

> the **W**est **C**oast   the **S**outheast   **s**outhern Iowa   **e**astern Pennsylvania

Capitalize the names of streets and highways as well as the names of specific sites, such as buildings, bridges, and monuments.

> **M**artin **L**uther **K**ing **J**r. Boulevard   **S**ears **T**ower   Lincoln **M**emorial

■ A. Identifying Place Names

Underline the correct use of the words in parentheses.

1. My family is from (harlem county, Harlem County).

2. That is located in (central, Central) Texas.

3. When I was five, we moved to the (midwest, Midwest).

4. We have a house on the beach of (lake, Lake) Michigan.

5. Unfortunately, the house is next to the (cleveland freeway, Cleveland Freeway).

■ B. Capitalizing Place Names

In the following sentences, circle the lowercase letters that should be capitalized.

1. The country of papua new guinea lies just north of australia.

2. Its capital city is port moresby.

3. Nearby islands, such as admiralty, new ireland, new britain, and bougainville, are part of the country.

4. Scientists believe that the aborigines of australia came from new guinea.

5. People first came to new guinea over ten thousand years ago from asia through indonesia.

Name .... Class .... Date ....

| 18.4 | **Capitalizing Other Proper Nouns and Adjectives** |

Key Information

Proper nouns are names of individual persons, places, things, or ideas. Proper adjectives are formed from proper nouns. All proper adjectives must be capitalized.

Italian cooking   Spanish rice

Capitalize the names of institutions, businesses, organizations, and clubs. Capitalize brand names, but not the words following them.

Goodwill Industries   Cub Scouts   Top Flight sneakers

Capitalize the names of historical events, periods, and documents.

Russian Revolution   Renaissance

Capitalize the names of days of the week, months of the year, and holidays, but do not capitalize seasons.

April   Memorial Day   Wednesday   summer

Capitalize the first and last words and all other important words in the titles of films, books, magazines, stories, songs, and the like.

"The Three Bears"   *A Tale of Two Cities*

Capitalize the names of ethnic groups, nationalities, and languages.

Asian   American   Colombian   French

■ A. Recognizing Proper Nouns and Proper Adjectives

Underline the correct use of the term in parentheses.

1. My brother and I are both (spanish, Spanish).

2. My favorite dessert is Carlsbad (Ice Cream, ice cream).

3. Patrick Henry signed the (declaration of independence, Declaration of Independence).

4. Have you seen the latest issue of (*rolling stone, Rolling Stone*)?

■ B. Capitalizing Proper Nouns and Proper Adjectives

In the following sentences, circle lowercase letters that should be capitalized.

1. Nan told us about her travels to european cities.

2. She knows a great deal about the french revolution.

3. She was there for bastille day, france's most important holiday.

4. Charles Dickens's book *a tale of two cities* is about the french revolution.

Name .... Class .... Date ....

19.1   Using the Period and Other End Marks

Key Information

Different end marks are used with different types of sentences. Use a **period** at the end of a statement (declarative sentence) or at the end of a command or a request (imperative sentence).

> This bus goes to the library. [declarative]
> Look out the window. [imperative]

Use a **question mark** at the end of a question (interrogative sentence).

> Why did you close the window?

Use an **exclamation point** at the end of a sentence that expresses a strong feeling (exclamatory sentence). Use an exclamation point at the end of a word or phrase that expresses a strong feeling and that stands alone outside of a sentence (interjection).

> What a great day we had!   Holy cow!   Gosh!

■ Using End Marks

The following passage describes a trip to the mall. Insert the missing periods, exclamation points, and question marks.

1. Oki asked her mother, "Since it's raining, can we go to the mall _____ "

2. "Fantastic _____ " replied Oki's mother _____ "I need to pick up some items at the mall _____ However, will you promise to clean your room if I take you with me _____ "

3. "Absolutely _____ " shrieked Oki _____ "Where is the broom _____ "

4. At the mall, Oki and her mother got separated _____ "Have you seen a dark-haired girl carrying several packages _____ " Oki's mother asked the security guard _____

5. "Not lately," replied the guard _____ "I'll keep a watch for her though _____ "

6. Just then Oki's mother heard a voice _____ "Wait _____ Here I am _____ " cried Oki _____ "What a great sale I found _____ "

7. "I should have known," sighed Oki's mother _____ "Did you buy anything _____ "

8. "Yes _____ " replied Oki excitedly _____ "I bought you a red umbrella _____ Now we won't get separated because I'll be able to see your umbrella in a crowd _____ "

9. "I don't carry an umbrella in the mall though, Oki," said Oki's mother _____

10. "That's right," sighed Oki _____ "I'm glad I saved the receipt _____ "

Name .... Class .... Date ....

| 19.2 | Using Commas I-A |

Key Information

Use a comma to signal a pause or separation between parts of a sentence. If a sentence contains three or more items in a series, separate the items with commas.

> Harold brought his hamster, his turtle, and his tarantula to school. [a series of nouns]
> The hamster slept, ate a carrot stick, and then ran around in its exercise wheel. [a series of verbs]

Use a comma to show a pause after an introductory word.

> Yes, the tarantula was a little scary.
> Well, I guess it was okay to bring the tarantula.

■ A. Using Commas in a Series and After an Introductory Word

Place commas where they are needed in these sentences.

1. Mary George and Flora rode the bus to school each day.

2. Mary always read a book wrote a letter or told stories on the way.

3. George and Flora studied history math and science together.

4. Do you think other students were disturbed bothered or annoyed by Flora?

5. No they were busy with their own work.

6. When they got to school, the students went to English class math class and history class.

■ B. Using Commas Correctly

Add commas where necessary in the following paragraph.

Henry Tom Renata and Julio like to play music together. Renata has a piano. Henry Tom and Julio bring pots wooden spoons plastic tubes a triangle a rain-maker or whatever they want to Renata's house. Renata dances sings and plays melody on the piano. Henry Tom and Julio play accompanying percussion. Well sometimes they even record their music on a tape recorder. Sometimes they listen to their tape rework parts they don't like and record again.

Name .... Class .... Date ....

| **19.2** | **Using Commas I-B** |

Key Information

Use a comma after two or more prepositional phrases at the beginning of a sentence. You need not use a comma after a single prepositional phrase, but it is not incorrect to do so.

> At the sound of the starting gun, the racers set off. [two prepositional phrases]
> From the start I knew who would win. [one prepositional phrase]

Use commas to mark interruptions in a sentence.

> Maria, without a doubt, was the fastest runner.
> Kevin was, of course, surprised to come in second.

If you use a name in direct address, use commas to set the name off from the rest of the sentence.

> Tell me, Fred, about your vacation.
> Hiram, did you go anywhere?

■ Using Commas with Prepositional Phrases, Interruptions, and Direct Address

Insert commas where they are needed in the following sentences. If a sentence is correct, write *correct*.

1. With a cry of relief he fell into his friend's arms._____

2. A vast array of life lives in the ocean. _____

3. Ms. Francis left for another school. _____

4. At the beginning of the game I was uncertain of my role._____

5. Because of circumstances beyond our control we were unable to compete. _____

6. My problem of course was that I had forgotten all about the test. _____

7. On the count of three everyone took off._____

8. Will you be coming with us Frank? _____

9. After driving all this way without a problem we found the gates closed. _____

10. Before six o'clock in the morning we had to be ready to leave._____

11. Peter are you going to finish your dinner?_____

12. After the game against the champs the coach congratulated each of us._____

13. With a nod of his head he rose up the chimney. _____

14. Excuse me Ms. Peterson but is this right? _____

15. On the day before the test Stu reviewed his notes._____

Name .... Class .... Date ....

| 19.3 | **Using Commas II-A** |

Key Information

Use a comma before *and, or,* or *but* when they join simple sentences to form a **compound sentence.**

Joseph Caulfield won the spelling bee, and he had the best grades in the school.
Joseph reads at the library most weekends, or he writes at his computer.
Joseph works hard, but he also plays soccer every other day.

■ Using Commas with Compound Sentences

Rewrite the following sentences, adding commas as needed. If the sentence is correct, write *correct.*

1. I looked in the closet and in the basement for my catcher's mitt. _____
   _____

2. Louis rode bareback for a while but later he switched to an English saddle._____
   _____

3. Everyone looked up but they soon turned back to the game. _____
   _____

4. The weather had begun to change or I was coming down with a cold._____
   _____

5. All the new players had new sneakers but the rest of us still played better._____
   _____

6. This book is not too long and it is very exciting._____
   _____

7. Have you ever been fishing in a lake or ocean? _____
   _____

8. Kellen stood up and walked quickly away but Steve stayed put. _____
   _____

9. Does Harold always borrow your book or does he have his own?_____
   _____

10. I let go of the line and the kite sailed away. _____
    _____

Name .... Class .... Date ....

| **19.3** | **Using Commas II-B** |

Key Information

Use a comma after the salutation in a personal letter and after the closing in both personal letters and business letters.

    Dear Sally,   Dearest Jorge,   Sincerely,   Best regards,

Use a comma to prevent misreading.

    After Susan called George came home.   After Susan called, George came home.
    In the forest fires are dangerous.   In the forest, fires are dangerous.

■ A. Using Commas to Prevent Misreading

Rewrite the sentences, inserting commas where needed to prevent misreadings.

  1. As I mounted the horse tried to bolt. _____

  2. When Enrique painted Valerie left the room. _____

  3. When I called Harry told me to come over. _____

  4. After Marta left the party was boring. _____

  5. Going down the escalator stopped. _____

  6. On the television news was being reported. _____

  7. Still running Jack made it on time. _____

  8. After reading Todd sat back down. _____

■ B. Using Commas in Letters

Write a short letter to a friend who is on vacation for the summer. Tell about all the things you will share when you get back together. Remember to use commas in the personal salutation and closing.

_____

_____

_____

_____

_____

_____

_____

_____

_____

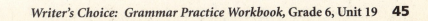

Name .... Class .... Date ....

19.4   Using Commas III-A

> **Key Information**
>
> If a date contains the month, day, and year, use commas before and after the year.
>
> Hiram was born on June 19, 1983, in Detroit.
>
> Do not use a comma if the date consists of only the month and the year.
>
> Hiram was born in June 1983 in Detroit.
>
> If the name of a state or country is used with the name of a city, place commas before and after the state or country.
>
> Hiram was born in Detroit, Michigan, but grew up in Caracas, Venezuela.
>
> Do not use a comma after the state if it is followed by a ZIP code.
>
> Hiram's address is 842 Bellflower Lane, Bexley, OH 43209.

■ A. Correcting Commas in Dates and Addresses

Insert commas where needed in the sentences below. Write *correct* if the sentence is correct.

1. Jordan was born on August 29 1986. _____

2. I know three people who were born in July 1984. _____

3. Colin used to live in Seattle Washington but on September 13 1990 he moved to Santiago

Chile. _____

4. December 25 1979 is a special date in the history of Las Cruces New Mexico. _____

5. My father owns the dry cleaning store at 45 South Main Street Columbus GA 31902. _____

6. Did you know a company builds submarines in New London Connecticut? _____

7. Have you ever wanted to visit London England? _____

8. On February 29 1924 my grandfather first met my grandmother in Tokyo Japan. _____

■ B. Using Commas in Dates and Addresses

Imagine that you have just moved to a new city. Write a short letter to your best friend telling him or her about the move. Be sure to include the date and your new address. Use additional paper if necessary.

_____

_____

_____

_____

_____

Name .... Class .... Date ....

19.4 Using Commas III-B

Key Information

If an abbreviated title or degree follows a person's name, separate the title or degree from the name and the rest of the sentence with commas.

Enrique Pasqual, Ph.D., opened his business next to his wife's office.

Use a comma before *too* when it means "also."

The Pasquals' daughter is a doctor, too.

Use a comma or a pair of commas to set off a direct quotation.

"Maybe," Ms. Pasqual replied, "but a plumber would be nice, too."

■ A. Using Commas with Titles

Insert commas where necessary in the sentences below. Write *correct* if the sentence needs no changes.

1. Did you get a letter from Morgan T. King M.D. too? _____

2. Kwan received a call from Joseph E. Conrad Ph.D. about his application. _____

3. Consuela wondered why the sign read David Jones M.A. when the office belonged to her sister too. _____

4. Greg's dentist is Julian P. Sands, D.D.S. _____

5. Terrance's dog received a shot from John K. Lands D.V.M. _____

6. The letter was addressed to Benjamin Diego Esq. _____

■ B. Using Commas with Direct Quotations

Insert commas to punctuate these sentences correctly.

1. "In the first place" Gertrude began "we don't have to tell you anything."

2. The detective paused a moment before replying "That's right, you don't."

3. "But I can promise you" he continued "that a trip downtown will only delay the inevitable."

4. Lawrence said from the couch "Oh, let's just get it over with."

5. "Keep quiet, Lawrence" Gertrude interrupted "or you'll get us all into hot water."

6. "Don't you realize Gertrude" Lawrence replied "that if the detective learns the whole story, he might be able to help us?"

Name .... Class .... Date ....

19.5   Using Semicolons and Colons

Key Information

Use a **semicolon** to form a compound sentence when a conjunction such as *and, or,* or *but* is not used.

    Jeffrey began piano lessons at age four**;** now, at age twelve, he is a virtuoso.

Use a **colon** to introduce a list of items that ends a sentence.

    Jeffrey has played in these European countries**:** France, Luxembourg, and Switzerland.

Never use a colon immediately following a verb or a preposition. A colon separates the hour and the minute when you write the time of day,

    Jeffrey practices every day at 6**:**15 A.M. and at 4**:**30 P.M.

Use a colon after the salutation of a business letter.

    Dear Madam**:**   Dear Ms. Freed**:**

■ A. Using Semicolons and Colons

Add semicolons and colons where needed in the sentences below. If the sentence is correct, write *correct*.

1. Julio played guitar, piano, drums, and saxophone. _____

2. The driver started his engine the race began at 1057 P.M. _____

3. After hiking twenty miles, the troop made camp they were all fast asleep by

730 P.M. _____

4. Hilda called softly to these three boys Miguel, Jorge, and Francis.

_____

■ B. Using Semicolons and Colons in Formal Letters

Add semicolons and colons where needed in the following letter.

Dear Dr. Goldstein

    Thank you very much for agreeing to meet with me about the class project. As I stated on the phone, I can be at your office at any one of the following three times 1130 A.M. Tuesday, 100 P.M. Tuesday, or 1100 A.M. Wednesday. The project will be due on the following Monday I hope you will be able to help me complete it in time. I want to talk with you about these diseases leukemia, sickle-cell anemia, and lupus.

                         Sincerely,

                         Yolanda Blanco

Name .... Class .... Date ....

| **19.6** | **Using Quotation Marks and Italics** |

Key Information

Place quotation marks before and after a direct quotation.

   "Ghana is located on the southwest coast of Africa," Chan explained.

Separate a phrase such as *he added* from the quotation with a comma. The comma appears outside opening quotation marks but inside closing quotation marks.

   "It covers about 92,000 square miles," he said, "which is roughly the size of Oregon."

Use quotation marks for the title of a short story, essay, poem, song, magazine or newspaper article, or book chapter.

   "My Last Duchess" [poem]   "Battle Hymn of the Republic" [song]
   "Punctuation" [book chapter]

Italics (underlining) should be used for the title of a book, play, film, television series, magazine, or newspaper.

   The Empire Strikes Back [film]   *Washington Post* [newspaper]   *Life* [magazine]

■ A. Punctuating Titles

Add quotation marks or underlining (for italics) where appropriate in the following sentences. The type of title is identified in parentheses.

  1. I looked everywhere for a copy of My Dinner with André (film).

  2. Mary mentioned that The Blue Hotel (short story) was her favorite story.

  3. Have you heard No Matter Where (song) yet?

  4. The lead story this morning was Mayor Wins Reelection (newspaper story).

  5. Do you still watch reruns of Leave It to Beaver (television show)?

  6. The assignment for the week was to read The Door into Time (book).

■ B. Using Quotation Marks

Add quotation marks, commas, and punctuation where needed in the sentences below. If the sentence is correct, write *correct*.

  1. Katherine said she was feeling a bit ill today. _____

  2. Her mother asked Do you need to stay home from school _____

  3. I don't think so Katherine replied There's a quiz I can't miss _____

  4. Well said her mom if you start to feel worse, have the nurse call me _____

  5. Katherine assured her that she would. _____

  6. Ms. Romano, Katherine's teacher, said You look a bit pale, Katherine _____

Name .... Class .... Date ....

19.7 Using Apostrophes and Hyphens

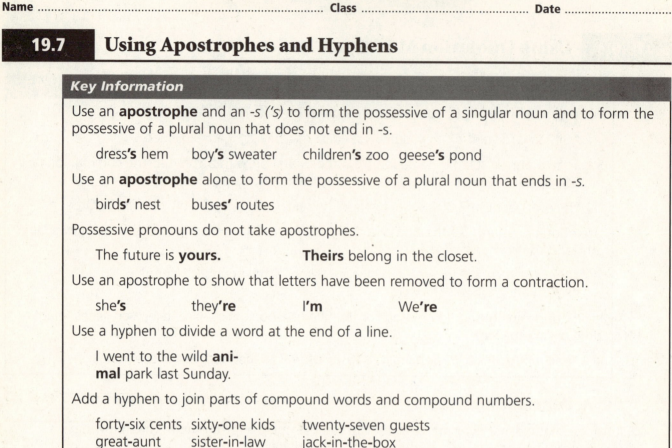

Key Information

Use an **apostrophe** and an *-s* (*'s*) to form the possessive of a singular noun and to form the possessive of a plural noun that does not end in -s.

    dress**'s** hem   boy**'s** sweater   children**'s** zoo geese**'s** pond

Use an **apostrophe** alone to form the possessive of a plural noun that ends in *-s.*

    bird**s'** nest   buse**s'** routes

Possessive pronouns do not take apostrophes.

    The future is **yours.**   **Theirs** belong in the closet.

Use an apostrophe to show that letters have been removed to form a contraction.

    she**'s**   they**'re**   I**'m**   We**'re**

Use a hyphen to divide a word at the end of a line.

    I went to the wild **ani-**
    mal park last Sunday.

Add a hyphen to join parts of compound words and compound numbers.

    forty-six cents sixty-one kids   twenty-seven guests
    great-aunt   sister-in-law   jack-in-the-box

■ A. Using the Possessive Form

Write the possessive form of the word in parentheses in the blank.

  1. The class visited the (children) zoo. _____

  2. Did you borrow (Chris) bike? _____

  3. Kevin spends a lot of time in the (carpenter) shop._____

  4. Picking up litter is (everyone) responsibility._____

  5. Did you find all the (birds) nests? _____

■ B. Using Apostrophes and Hyphens

Rewrite the sentences below, placing apostrophes and hyphens where needed.

  1. Youve got only forty five minutes to complete your assignment. _____

     _____

  2. How do you know if its time to go when your watch seems to be badly broken?

     _____

  3. My great aunt will be seventy five on Friday._____

  4. My sister in law will be twenty one on Saturday. _____

Name .... Class .... Date ....

19.8 Using Abbreviations

Key Information

Use **abbreviations** for a person's title and for any professional or academic degree that follows a name.

    Henrietta Jordan, **M.D.**   **Ms.** Taylor   Harold Solus, **Ph.D.**

Some organizations and government agencies are abbreviated. Use capital letters and no periods.

    United Nations—**UN**   National Football League—**NFL**

The abbreviations A.M. and P.M. are used with times of day. Dates often contain the abbreviations B.C. (before Christ) and A.D. (*anno Domini,* in the year of the Lord).

    7:55 A.M.   310 B.C.   A.D. 667

Abbreviate days and months only in a list or chart. Abbreviate units of measure in scientific writing.

    Tues.   **Mar.**   Kilogram—**kg**   gallon—**gal.**   liter—**l**

Use the two-letter Postal Service abbreviations for the names of states.

    Alaska—**AK**   Maine—**ME**   Virginia—**VA**

■ A. Forming Abbreviations

Write the correct abbreviation for each of the following.

1. December _____

2. before Christ_____

3. Saturday_____

4. Virginia _____

5. liter _____

6. National Basketball Association _____

■ B. Using Abbreviations

Write in the blanks the abbreviation for the words in italics.

1. I signed the letter *Mister* Kenneth Dean. _____

2. Here is a note with Hiram's address: 126 Beech *Avenue.* _____

3. Maria found her height on the chart: six *feet.* _____

4. The sign read, "Closed *Wednesday* for Remodeling." _____

5. The letter was dated *October* 12, 1892. _____

6. The book was written in *the year of the Lord* 223. _____

7. I got home from the store at 8:30 *in the evening.*_____

8. Jessica got several maps from the *American Automobile Association.*_____

Name .... Class .... Date ....

19.9   Writing Numbers

Key Information

When you use numbers in sentences, spell out the numbers that you can write in one or two words.

 I saw that movie **three** times.
 The farm sets aside **one hundred** acres for the cows.
 My father owns **755** acres of farm land.

Write a very large number as a numeral followed by the word million or billion.

 The United States has a population of over **250 million.**

Spell out ordinal numbers (third, fourth, fifth, and so on). Use numerals to show the exact time. Otherwise, spell out the time of day,

 I get up at 7:15 A.M. I go to bed around **ten o'clock.**

Use numerals to show dates, house and street numbers, telephone numbers, amounts of money with more than two words, and percentages. Write out the word percent.

 page **7**   **$53.25**   **66** percent

■ Using Numerals and Numbers

Correct the use of numerals and numbers in the following sentences. If no changes need to be made, write *correct*.

1. Our first class started at nine-fifteen A.M. _____

2. We drove around the block 12 times looking for the right address. _____

3. I have twenty-six dollars and seventeen cents in the bank. _____

4. One billion people live in China. _____

5. There are over seven million people living in New York City. _____

6. I left tracks for 10 feet on my new bike. _____

7. We won sixty percent of our games this year. _____

8. Our school took 7th place in the national spelling bee. _____

9. Jeffrey answered 96 percent of the questions correctly. _____

10. Georgia is located about four hundred fifty miles south of Ohio. _____

11. Carrie started 101 books last summer. _____

12. Lois and Paul live at twenty-six Mulhullen Drive. _____